Good True Stories

GOOD TRUE STORIES

POEMS BY

ERIC TORGERSEN

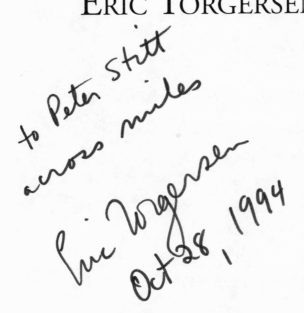

to Peter Stitt
across miles

Eric Torgersen
Oct 28, 1994

LYNX HOUSE PRESS
Amherst, Massachusetts / Portland, Oregon

ACKNOWLEDGEMENTS

Some of the poems in this volume appeared previously in periodicals as follows:

Black Fly Review: "Cat and Bridge," "Not Stopping"
CoEvolution Quarterly: "Getting My Punch Back," "Good True Story"
Dacotah Territory: "Owl Gift"
Green River Review: "Already Dead"
Hanging Loose: "Taking Tickets," "I've Come To Be One Who Cries"
Ironwood: "My Blindness," "Praise of Hunger, Praise of Food," "The Man Who
    Broke Up the Dinner Party Answers," "Villanelle of The Final Report,"
    "Killing the Milk Snakes," "A Story"
Jeopardy: "Open Stage Poetry Reading"
Literary Review: "Sons and Fathers: Ashbery," "Of What Remains"
New Letters: "Staying"
Notus: "The Throne of the Third Heaven of the Nations Millennium General
    Assembly"
Passages North: "The Lone Rangers Rides Off"
Poetry Now: "Love on the Friendship Quilt"
River Styx: "After Rilke," "Things Die"
waves: "Up Here (Again)"

"A Story," "I've Come to be One Who Cries," and "My Blindness," appeared in
    The Third Coast, Wayne State University Press

"Not Stopping," appeared in *Contemporary Michigan Poetry,* Wayne State
    University Press

Copyright © 1994 by Eric Torgersen
Design by Christopher Howell
Cover Art by Jósef Kovács

Library of Congress Cataloging-in-Publication Data

Torgersen, Eric, 1943 –
        Good true stories : poems / by Eric Torgersen.
            p. cm.
        ISBN 0-89924-090-9 : $9.95
        I. Title.
    PS3570.068G66   1994
    811'.54—dc20
                                                        94-25549
                                                        CIP

Printed by Chester Press, Inc., Emporia, Kansas for:

Lynx House Press
Box 640
Amherst, MA 01002

and

9305 SE Salmon Ct.
Portland, Oregon 87216

Lynx House Press books are distributed by Small Press Distribution, 1814 San
Pablo Ave., Berkeley, CA 94702.

for Ann

who reminds me to live

Table of Contents

Section Three   / 45

one

Staying

It's your birthday,
the surprise
party you wanted so hard
you asked for it—

and here you are
in the bathroom
rubbing tears away.

Through the door,
you hear someone
ask someone in a whisper
what's the matter?

Now stand, face
yourself
in the mirror,
wash your hands
and face and tuck
your shirt in better,
check your eyes
again, and open

to the nervous,
kind smiles
of your friends.

Now search
in their eyes,
find an arm
you can touch,
take a drink,
let them know
with a look
that you'll be staying.

Of What Remains

Of what remains I've made one perfect hermit,
lean as I've grown fat in your good presence,
austere as all the absence of our comforts,
in a plain gray shack on land we're leaving empty.
Each lost part of me that you remember,
that found no home in our household, is with him.
The few spare loaves left over from our baking,
the scatter of fish too thin for our wide net,
won't feed the wishful others who come and go,
finding not enough hunger there to hold them.
They bring him just enough for the simple work
he does there, where our travels content him to stay.
This is my invitation: imagine that place.
If you were gone, that's where I'd go and live.

Up Here

Even in my life
gravity can fail,

I float up here where there's nothing
to hold on to, and nothing holds back.

It's crowded. There's music and smoke.
You make the rules.

It's the heaven the Old West went to
when it died.

My name, the house, and you
are rocks in my pocket.

     *

Driving alone, cross-country,
on the empty Interstates,

by radio, you know
you could do anything.

Look, there's a hitchhiker.
Look, there's a Holiday Inn.

You're in space.
You're on the high seas

and life stories
have a ten mile limit.

     *

I see blood. I think everyone's face
is covered with blood.

But you're tripping, remember?

I'm not hungry. Everyone's hungry, and
eating everyone else until everyone's
inside everyone else but there's nothing
there, it's transparent, they just go
through. No one's there.

But you're tripping, remember?

*

Americans say *Go for broke*
and *That was a close one.*

We say *Don't kid yourself,*
Double or nothing, Dumb luck.

We talk ourselves up
and back down into our lives.

Look: I'm OK. Don't worry.
I know what I'm doing. You know *me:*

I'm Saint Francis. I live here.
I love you. I have work to do.

For Ann With Pictures

In the old home movie you dance for just your father
on the sidewalk in front of a hotel in downtown Chicago:
five years old, already in ballet slippers,
all alone with your father in that city,
not having to think there's anything wrong in dancing.
I've felt the way your dancing made him feel,
and what can a father do then but get pictures?
But suppose in that film I had to play the cop
who comes and says *No dancing on the sidewalk*
ever again for the eighty years you have left?
I'd want arthritis in my knees and fingers.
Never stop, and that won't have to happen.
That girl's inside you; you've become her mother.
She's still dancing. Let me take your picture.

Owl Gift

Today I go nowhere:
car and road blown away
somewhere deep in the snow

a sparrow clings
to the lee of the feeder
others hunch deep
in the bony forsythia

I have food, dry heat
and work enough to keep me

deep last night
I switched on the light outside
and got a bird for you:

small dark kitten
of an owl in the snow
by the door

it would swivel its head
a slow and seamless half-circle
and back to me

it flew away only
when I went for the book
to name it:

screech-owl, the one
small owl with ear-tufts

the one
small necessary gift
so deep in winter

Love on the Friendship Quilt

Roll me in designer sheets, the song from the sexy movie says,
but now it's love on wedding sheets from cousins, sensible JC
    Penney sheets;
now it's love on the friendship quilt, with a block from Mother and
    Father at the center,
with blocks from Peter & Ilah, Smythe & Irma, the Elmer Riggles,
from Oscar & Velma, Herb & Martha, Mr. and Mrs. H. Wischmeyer;
on the friendship quilt it's love with the lights on, it's legal, it's love
    without whiskey, without perfume;
on the quilt it's a square dance with the same old partner and caller,
the same band's same few tunes in the same old Grange Hall;
it's for keeps on the quilt, for kids, it's for the country,
you dig, on the quilt, deep down for the one good reason
you came here, kept coming back, will keep on coming.

Good True Story

Here's a good true story. Once, before payday, when I had no money and needed a pack of cigarettes—that's right, cigarettes. There was a jar in town, the coffee money at work, a few coins, only coffee money anyway; I could even tell my friends and they would laugh.

There were two different ways of walking into town, and I went the way that passed a little warehouse. A man called out, do you want to make a buck? I didn't think at first he was talking to me. I carried my end of a sofa onto a van. He probably thought I wouldn't take his money, but it was better than coffee money any day, and this is the truth: I haven't stolen much since.

It's a story I tell to friends, but I've been thinking. The price of a story like that has gone through the roof, the way prices of gold and silver sometimes do, and people start selling everything they have left.

I'm trying to say, I'd convert it to Jesus Christ. I mean, convert to Jesus and tell that story. It really could have been Jesus who gave me that dollar, though I didn't think to notice what he looked like. A story like that, they put you right on TV.

If you hold out too long, the price could go back down.

Still, I might need it sometime, for myself, and it's no good for that once you sell it.

Or someone could turn up later whose money is better.

If you turn on the TV someday and it's me with my story, you'll know I sold before the bottom dropped out. For now, I'm keeping the story, to sell to friends, I mean, to *tell*. A man can't just tell everything he owns, can he? I mean, he can't just *sell*.

Getting My Punch Back

It felt good! An afternoon digging out logs we'd let the snow bury. Inside again, I threw off some clothes and made a sandwich. I caught myself making muscles in the mirror, and throwing my punch. Take *that*. My punch!

When I was young, I'd fight out romantic fistfights in the living room. Take *that*. My mother couldn't stand it. In real life I've never thrown my punch, not once. I fought my last fight in seventh grade, when I goosed Frank DiFede, a Deer Park kid who had to ride the Melville bus. He turned on me and I handed my books to Ann Quick, saying *Hold these*. We wrestled. I'd misjudged Frank DiFede—a boy can grow fast in seventh grade—but the bus driver got there in time.

Later, anyone could see I wasn't the fistfighting kind. I could even tell Eddie Young he was full of shit, when he leaned on Seri LoDato in the locker room, and you should have seen Eddie Young.

Even today I'm exempt—invisible to anyone looking for a fight. It's a good way to be, mostly; sometimes it hurts my foolish pride.

I'd long since forgotten my punch, and now here it is: an old friend I have nothing left in common with. Just a Sunday punch, an old habit, a body's nostalgia. But why now? Take *that*. I'm needed? Somebody needs me?

Taking Tickets

A woman in her forties, dressed wealthy, stands by the door for a while and then says, You couldn't let me in for twenty minutes, could you, I shouldn't even ask, it's just that I'd be leaving in twenty minutes and I'd like to go in, it seems a shame to get a ticket for twenty minutes, it wouldn't be right for you to let me in though, would it, that's right, I'm sorry, I shouldn't ask. . . . She walks away fast.

I like her; she tells the truth and she doesn't want anything free.

A girl in shorts and halter top, barefoot, pretty, stands for a while—they all start out wrong that way, standing a while without talking to get up their nerve— then tells me she's been waiting for weeks, looking forward, her friends are inside, a bummer, could she just sneak in? I give her my smile of apology, gee, I'm just here taking tickets, after all. . . . She knows how I feel, but her friends, looking forward, a bummer, oh well. . . . She says have a good day.

I like her too, she's nice. If I like you I won't let you in without a ticket.

There's never a problem with friends, they always have tickets, and they've got them out before you have to ask.

A guy who worked here, inside, but he quit or they fired him, walks up and starts to small talk. Nice day. Good crowd? I give him short answers, I know what he wants. He never looks straight at me once, just asks his questions. How's Bob? Did Annette have her baby yet? He doesn't want to have to ask, he wants me to say come on in Ed? On me? We were never friends, I'm going to make him say it. And it takes him so long, he can think of so many questions. Finally he asks, says he's broke, I say go on in, but

19

no smile, no friendship, just get out of here. Ten minutes of thank you till I say again go on in.

Just make me despise you, you can get me to let you in free. I do it to hurt you.

I don't know why I've stayed at this job for so long. It's not the right kind of job for someone like me.

I stay because sometimes somebody just walks through. They have no ticket and I don't ask, they don't need one. It's not just beautiful women or old men with canes; it's people who don't need tickets, who walk right through. It's like they hypnotize me, but they don't. It's who they are. I don't ask for a ticket, I say hi.

What I wonder about, what amazes me, is how do they know they don't need tickets? You need tickets here. People cheat and sneak, but it's not the same thing. What would it feel like, knowing you don't need a ticket? They never act like movie stars, or the president; more like they don't know anyone needs a ticket. But they do know that. They don't act embarrassed, either.

That's what taking tickets is all about. It can take months, even years, till someone walks through, but it makes you feel good, deep inside, way down, all the way.

Killing the Milk Snakes

It couldn't be true, about them drinking from cows,
but milk snakes do like to live in the walls of houses.
You call them house snakes. Ours would sun
In the grass right off the front porch on warm days
and slide up under the siding home at night.

It felt good, letting milk snakes come and go,
watching our step around that part of the lawn,
and I didn't mind when a baby snake was crawling
on the kitchen floor in the morning early one spring.

Then we found a dead skin on the living room rug.
I'm not sure why, but it meant we had to kill them.
It's hard to kill snakes you've talked about in poems,
and I'd said "not to appeal is that milk snake"—
something at home in life that doesn't complain.

I dropped a concrete block off the porch on the first one.
I thought it would leap and hiss and scare me sick
but it never said a word, just made for home,
up under the siding, with a kink where a corner of the block
must have hit. It had a hard time to get that kink
through the hole, and two days later it started to stink.

My wife said I didn't know how to kill a snake right.

I cut the other one down with a hoe. I could see it
sliding off home already, really slow,
the way a snake has of looking like it's not there.
With a hoe you can keep a snake from running away.

First I took off a little piece of the tail,
then three more pieces. Here are my observations:
Down to six inches, that snake never made a move
that wasn't classic. I'm writing a loose pentameter;
if you're going to write in prose you might as well.
I started this poem before I started the killing—
which would you start first, with that much choice left?
I'm tired of the killing we do to keep these houses.

My Blindness

Once I woke up in the dark and thought I was blind. There was no light at all. There's always *some* light.

Blind, I was calm in that perfect dark. Friends would come, and I'd tell them what they had had to do. It would be all right.

I'd go back home, but *dignified,* and I'd know my way perfectly in the house, even on the streets. I'd only been gone a few years.

I'd have them read me strange books, and they'd love my strangeness, thinking *This is what it was, we knew there was something.* They'd loved it a little already.

There at home in my great dark I'd find a single purpose, and begin.

But you know this: the light came.

Don't laugh at me. I live with so little blindness. Such a long way I've come; so little blindness.

I've Come to be One Who Cries

—for Bob Hershon

I've come to be one who cries when the plane the guys built in shop class on the TV news is going to fly and everyone's there, parents, little kids, the teachers not even dressed up, the mayor and the principal making speeches, the shop teacher saying these are real fine boys, the guys standing round saying *it's gonna crash*, putting their arms around girls and the teachers don't stop them, the band playing the school song while the pilot gets in and checks everything out like you're supposed to, finally kicks it over and taxies to the end of the runway with a drum roll and everybody screaming already, and it goes off the line like a dragster and takes off! The band starts "Off we go, into the wild blue yonder," and the guys are slapping five and grabbing girls and telling each other *it flies! that piece of shit flies!*

two

Not Stopping

I have no place to go inside this mood,
but make no place for anyone riding shotgun.

You have the road, your thumb and sign,
an errand at a named place on the map;

I have this truck, mood, momentum, this nothing
to stop me, this no place to go.

Interstate

Your life's a pothole on the Interstate:
Left too long, you'd let the dirt get through.
They'll be along to fix you. Sit and wait.

It's your fault when the shipment gets there late;
Sure it works, but still, it isn't *new*.
Your life's a pothole on the Interstate.

When men in nylon suits are at the gate,
Don't be flattered that they came to you.
You don't fit in their plans. Sit tight and wait,

And please don't sign. You're blighted real estate
To them, for tearing down. You spoil the view.
Your life's a pothole on the Interstate.

They live at such remove: their miles of fate.
From so far off they can't see what they do.
That makes chances; stay alert and wait.

Their children void the future they'd create:
Bright and eager, soft, uncertain, *few*,
They range in fierce new cars the Interstate
In search of something, as you sit and wait.

The Lone Ranger Rides Off

Thank God he's gone,
on his horse
of all colors—

we can take up again
the lives
he rode shooting into

in the blind
mask of belief
in the legend of himself—

and why should we have
to think we've failed him?
ransomed

these lives of ours,
let him ride off
with his guns and his needs

into other lives,
quiet as ours,
further west—

why should a woman
blame herself
for not knowing how to offer

what would ease him
down
off the horse of his differences?

Why this guilt—
we can't spit it out—
for all he will learn

when the bright
horse fails
beneath him,

when he comes,
hat in hand, palefaced,
blinking

in our daily sun,
for our blessing,
for a place among us?

A Story

The ending is this:
the one true friend comes back
and you live in the place in the woods
as you promised each other you would.

Everyone else
in the story is parents.
They make you go to school;
you come out parents.

That's when the friend ran away.

For years in the story
you're alone.
Every new friend
ends up trying to make you eat breakfast.
Ends up getting married.

This is the place in the story
where you lose hope.

The Hut, When It Falls

The usual story of damage to a child:
a girl, denied a place in the wooden hut
her brothers (in father's presence) built, goes out
to build her own; it falls; unable to build
a hut to house a doll, she falls to tears
she is too proud, so young, to hide, even from father.
Later she marries, much later gives birth to a daughter,
not asking approval, having waited so many years.
But that child weeps inside her even now,
the hut she built still trembles, poised to fall,
from father (and husband) hidden all too well,
darker down than any marriage vow.
And where will she turn? To see the trembling stilled
lest the hut, when it falls, unhouse the actual child.

The Man Who Broke Up the Dinner Party
Answers

It made me feel small, like a husband,
and I never married, never owned

a table worth turning over, china
worth shattering, linen worth blood

from the cut hand I sucked and cursed
and wrapped in a torn shirt, in a pocket.

Can't they make it new again, those bees,
those communist women at their weaving?

It was only the long lines, the slow,
enforced pace, solemnity, cold white glitter;

I was only too proud to eat cold history,
to stand in the breadlines at the tomb;

I only declined the feast in the mausoleum
as Yesenin did, who wrote his regrets in blood.

Praise of Hunger, Praise of Food

1

It was not the end of eating look we eat
to speak of it was not the end of speaking
but they are new our eating and our speech
this melon is new and the word is new   *melón*

since after seventy days we came off the mountain
having eaten the flesh of strangers and of friends

the potato is new and *papa* the flesh of the cow
is new and our eyes are new having seen such eyes
having seen them we turn away from your old eyes
your old words   yours who will never eat this *melón*

2

Yes we converts after all were blessed
who knew a god even yours when we tasted one
who needed a god as man and woman need
and so the old gods never wholly left us

not those who lived on the memory of our gods
as the prisoner refusing food lives on its memory

and look now here it is you whose god is a memory
who are offered the body now of a god that comes
who lie down with memory now or rise and walk
across the room to the table and take and eat

Villanelle of the Final Report

I don't want the bodies of my kids and a lie,
said one of the mothers who stood by the palace door.
I want to know who killed them and why.

The country was besieged by a huge and hidden army,
said the government's final report on the "dirty war."
Take, eat, it said, these bodies and this lie.

One top Western diplomat told me
he thought the armed forces were trying to shore
up their ranks by not saying who killed, exactly, or why.

Not autonomous right wing death squads, but policy,
said the leading human rights activist, mourning a daughter.
They'd given him nothing to bury except the lie.

A former well-placed policeman who ran away
called it a pact of blood among young officers.
This seems to answer one question, but not why.

Unless the killers are judged, what happened here yesterday
will happen elsewhere tomorrow, continued the mother.
Alive in our bodies, elsewhere, we ponder the lie
and the fear of knowing exactly who killed them, and why.

Open Stage Poetry Reading

—for Mary Jo McBay

After the one that sings, and after the one
that can make up poems of a kind right on the spot;
after a girl who didn't . . . *walk* very well,
took five minutes to get from her seat to the stage
then read one poem with hardly any words in it
and halted the whole way back in a staggering silence;
after the bald one's rhymes about his teeth;
a woman got up whose poems won't write down,
it's all in the way the voices in her come out.

We went to a medium once, and a woman locked
in a trance let a dead man come inside her and talk.
She held herself like . . . a woman being a man.
That's what it was at the open stage poetry reading,
and I left without talking, I hadn't come expecting it.
What could I have told her, I think it's a dead man?
It wasn't something I wanted to get that close to.
I could never do it myself, let a dead man come in—
or would it be, into me, a dead woman that would come?

Already Dead

A crackpot gringo in Guatemala told me:
when the pilots of the suicide planes began
their dives down at the ships they were already dead.
Coming from him, a smug didactic metaphor.
Remember Joplin's "Mercedes Benz," on PEARL?
The reason we found the final chorus so moving
is that when she shouts *everybody!* but no one joins in
and she goes on singing alone she's already dead.
When John F. Kennedy took Marilyn Monroe in his arms,
each could tell that the other was already dead.
How they wept! It was love in a great tradition:
two corpses holding each other, crying *if only
I could live for your sake o my beloved.* They went
from that place bravely with deaths to finish for everyone.

Things Die

Auch die Dinge sterben sounds like Rilke.
Things fall off the table, down to chemistry.
For things, then, heaven really is *up* from here;
all a thing would need is escape velocity.
They've launched a few expensive things immortal;
only the radio dies after a while.
How save the soul from dying down to physics?
Why don't they shoot one soul, still locked in its thing,
all the way out to the empty where they could track it?
It's worth a try; if it works it's a pricy ticket.
The immortal souls of the rich enough to die
in space could weigh nothing forever in their vacuum,
blips on our mortal screens, not coming home
ever to die in the world and the way of things.

Sons and Fathers: Ashbery

First you get to be right for thirty years,
then you get to be wrong for thirty years.
(*First* you get twenty years as a virtuous pagan.)
This is the law of the conservation of rectitude.
Paraphrase: first the son, and then the father.
My friend your friend the Francois Villon of the seventies
said *we* and didn't mean me *must be our own children.*
He's his own father now. And then you die.
Thirty years of asking the old men *why*
are you doing that? Loving the way they look
at you: sorry, guilty, wrong. Then comes a day
you look up at the younger men advancing.
Just the look of them has you owing answers.
Right they are. You go on whittling your stick.

Cat and Bridge

I let the cat follow me home and that was wrong.
I didn't know what to do, and that was wrong,
so I just kept walking, and *that* was wrong.
It was so important, it went on happening and happening.

When I finally got to the bridge, the cat still following,
everything wrong, he said *there's a cat behind you*—
an old man with whiskers in a yellow rubber slicker
and hat and rubber boots was there on the bridge
looking real the way someone on television looks real.

It hadn't been raining. It didn't look like rain.
He looked so real. The next thing I did was wrong:
I said *it's all right* and kept walking, whatever he was.

By the time I was ready to look back the cat was gone;
I didn't look far enough back to see the man.
I wanted the cat back, almost. Once, in my bedroom,
up near the ceiling in a corner, a raccoon,
a comic strip coon with a mask on, looked right at me,
looked *real* at me over his shoulder, and walked away.

The Throne of the Third Heaven of the Nations Millennium General Assembly

1

Certainly no one thought of him
      as either a fanatic or a madman
James Hampton
son of a Baptist minister
described as timid, thin, bespectacled
who did custodial work
      for the General Services Administration
          St. James,
          Director of Special Projects
          for the State of Eternity
who told me he was working on something
      a sustained, intense, and solitary involvement
in an unheated garage
      that he rented for fifty dollars a month
and it might come to something some day
          This is true: that the Great Moses
          giver of the tenth commandment
          appeared in Washington
I'd see winos give him tinfoil, gold wrapping
cigarette and gum wrappers
tables and chairs, burnt-out lightbulbs
      glass jars, cardboard
and he'd give them nickels and dimes
          On October 21 1946
          the Star of Bethlehem appeared
          over our nation's capital
My brother came running to the store
      someone oughtta see this!
fifty thrones, pulpits, crowns

standards icons offertory tables
crowned by the words FEAR NOT
numerous references to the Book of Revelations
inscriptions in English and a secret personal script
　　　　that has not been been deciphered
　　　　　　Adam, the first man God created
　　　　　　appeared in Person on January 29 1949
　　　　　　the day of President Truman's Inauguration
Maybe he wanted to make a name for himself
　　　　in church circles
but now he's dead and it all comes to nothing
it seems to me an example
of the futility of life
said a man named Meyer Wertlieb
　　　　who owned a clothing store

a sister in South Carolina
　　　　who didn't want anything to do with it
a number of inquiries from prospective buyers
finally purchased by the Smithsonian Institution
　　　　a short distance from the garage
for a small sum of money
　　　　equal to back rent owed

2

James Hampton has not been deciphered
now he's dead as tinfoil

it all comes to nickels and dimes
from prospective buyers

it seems to me an example
of the futility of work
of vision of English
of symbols of cardboard

of sustained, intense
and solitary involvement

certainly no one thought of him
as either a minister or a brother

certainly no one thought of him
as *name* or *star* or *example*

but I'd see winos give him gold
I'd see winos in church

as symbols
symbols as clothing

and maybe he wanted
to make clothing for himself

maybe he wanted
to appear in Person

crowned by the words FEAR NOT
on the day of his Inauguration

3

THIS IS TRUE

That Adam Washington Moses St. James Hampton,
son and sum and example of secret light,

Director, Star and President of the Institution
for Services General and Special to the State of Eternity,

who described himself as created, owned and used
by the first true geometric God of nations,

in an unheated garage bespectacled himself
to see by the not burnt-out lightbulbs of solitary vision,

made inquiries into the Book of prospective Revelations,
where symbols are numerous, personal and equal,

and deciphered the tablets, icons and inscriptions
that appeared in patterns of light over timid Bethlehem.

three

False Prospector

The pick and spade are for show. You're a theoretician.
What you dig is gold by definition.

Dear Bob Dylan

I got your new album today. At least you're not dead,
like Elvis, and didn't we love you almost that badly?
The way the shit that shot John Lennon loved him?
I guess I've loved you like that. I'd never harm you.

Sure it hurt, to be dropped for some true believer,
younger, much less complex, we'll see how forgiving.
I must have become a threat when I lost the blind faith
you taught me by outguessing me all those years.

Now you want me back? We have to talk.
About Jesus, for one thing. Not the fact that you're Jewish;
I loved the scene in Scaduto's book where you learned
that Ramblin' Jack (whom you needed, then didn't need)
was the creature of Elliot Adnopoz, once of Brooklyn,
a doctor's bad son, self-created like you.
(You rolled on the floor of the Gaslight, laughing
          helplessly.)
The fact that we believe what keeps us working,
what else would we believe? You did good gospel.

Jesus is one of the opposites of irony,
the great black hole that almost sucked you in.
You couldn't write a line or sing a note
that wouldn't drown in all its implications,
which I spoiled you by understanding so completely.
Was that what turned you paranoid and strange,
one song a Jeremiad, the next a bitter shrug?

I never gave up; I know them all by heart.

A brilliant kid, you were so sincere it hurt.
Then, to face money, dope, reporters' questions,
followers who followed you all over,
you changed life stories, costumes, faces, voices,
threw them to us like Elvis throwing scarves.
Elvis whom you dreaded most becoming,
working crowds so starved they'd swallow anything:
swallow him stoned and fat, forgetting the words,
swallow him dead so hard they'd raise him up.

Haven't you known my answer all along?
Come back, if you want to. Save me again, if you can.

Dear Mr. Rilke

Welcome to America. Fans here love you so much
that every one of us translates all your poems
into our language, which somewhat resembles English.
None of us knows German, but we manage,
and we know you will too, with a positive attitude.

Someone who writes lyrics (we mean something different)
for the Grateful Dead (I'll try to explain them later)
has just released his version of your Elegies,
and I myself am writing your life as a musical
with songs like "Oh Clara" and "Military School Blues."

Even before you died, we invited you over,
naively, by gosh, but sincerely; you were amused.
Now that, like all the rest, you've come to live here,
even under posthumous circumstances,
it's my job to make you feel at home.

You'll be staying for a time at the Holiday Inn.
What castles we have are not yet ripe for ghosts,
but we have agents checking out condominiums:
everything clean and new, the way we like it.
The laundry machines in the basement require coins.

Once you've learned our language you'll be teaching
poetry workshops for the Dead Writers' School
at the Teachers' College—oops! The University.
Nice young kids who'll just admire you crazy.
Give them tips and keep them entertained.

Whenever you look like you need some cheering up
they'll want to take you out drinking at the bar;

whatever you choose to make of this opportunity
is all right with us, since you're famous, if it's
                discreet.
Please bear in mind that we have some new diseases.

(Young girls, I think? They're still your best bet here.)
Bringing the Mrs., we hope? The little girl?
Please let us know if there are child care requirements,
as we have waiting lists for that sort of thing,
and whether Mrs. Rilke has any hobbies.

Before I close, allow me to blurt out
how eager we are to read some American Rilke!
(It says in your file that you wrote some things in French
and it got you into trouble with the Germans—
leave them to us. We've got them by the balls.)

It's safe to say we'll all be making adjustments.
We know that you don't understand us, or welcome our love,
and wrestling foreign angels hurts our pride.
You kick our asses! (We die of your stronger being.)
We hope you'll try to keep our feelings in mind.

Dear Orpheus

Ovid says the Thracian women's grievance
was that you took your new bride's loss so hard
you couldn't look a woman in the eyes
and couldn't keep your hands off Thracian boys.
Naughty, I guess, but still: for that they stoned you,
tore you apart and threw your head in the river?
(And even that couldn't shut you all the way up.)
To the modern sensibility it seems
that everyone in the story was acting out:
you in sexy sulks, those women in violence.

Now, he says, you have her back, down there.
She walks behind; you're careful where your eyes go.
I don't suppose she'd let you try a comeback?
Afraid to trust you all alone up here
among the pretty living, those roving eyes
that made you fuck up last time still a threat?
All I can say is, we're in bad shape up here,
the whole top 40's choked on bubblegum,
and you could blow these New Kids right away.
How will we ever know unless you try?

Dear Former President Reagan

Thank you for winning the Cold War. Now that it's over
we can all relax, even here in Poetry Land
where we were with you every step of the way.
We won't forget you now that you've retired,
not even when the mopping up is done.
Pockets of diehard resistance were expected,
but soon we'll all be sitting around and singing,
one big family, darkies and all, like the old days
before Marx, Pound and Williams bombed Pearl Harbor.

Thanks for the right to celebrate a flower,
to lift new songs like kites to clear blue sky;
we've all got brand new shiteating nymph-and-shepherd
grins miles wide on our faces, and you're why;
we're choosing life like crazy in the bushes,
begetting Little Ponies that can fly.

Just a little taste of what they'll see
now that you've restored our will to sing.
Of course we're young; our voices are still changing;
as John Keats said, the best is yet to be.

Postcard: Dear Post-Structuralist Criticism

Thank you very much, but we knew it already.
We trust these words no further than we throw them;
all our far-fetched tricks to keep them put
are busywork, nostalgia, consolation.
Words, we can't forget, are waves *and* particles,
shrapnel from the Big Bang in the brain;
hence chaos and entropy are the very givens
from which we fly, toward which we gaily tend,
and needn't be mimicked by those in search of a style.

After Rilke

In America, sometimes, someone's only father
gets up from the table right in the middle of dinner,
jumps in the car and drives all the way out west

to be farther away from the great cathedrals of Europe.
He's heard that in parts of Alaska there's almost nothing.
To his children he might as well be dead.

The children, later, fly east to Europe on Fulbrights
to scan the tongues that tangled Grandfather's English
and photograph churches Father drove away from.

What Bears Repeating

There on stage was Elvis, stoned and fat,
flubbing the whispers on "Are You Lonesome Tonight?"—
weeks from death, alone up there facing us down,
laughing in all our faces how little it mattered.
Into our thousand faces in Rackham Hall
you chuckled "I read these because you expect me to"
and stumbled through "The Bear" and "Little Sleep's-Head."
(Later you came to what you had the heart for.)
Yeats makes that same crack on the Caedmon record,
then storms the water-dream-song a Thoreau-struck
Irish lad of century previous drowned
his London blues in, sears it with old man's breath,
shrivels it half to a curse. In death's own face
he sang a song to bear a life's repeating.

Rhymes, you reckon, are tracks we follow in snow
to places where someone else has already been:
The old horse walks, and bears in safety children
down its own tracks in same and dusty rings
while every poet rides for the frontier.
But the purest wanderer, paid to perform, re-enacts
in the Wild West Show his solo escapes, his kills,
while carousel horses rising and falling like breasts
weightless in the circles of their music
bear the children in their brightness up.
Rhyme for song then, song to bear the children,
song to bear repeating unto death
in what's become of the old New World we had
where each man found his own new place to die.

Orpheus on Translation

Rilke noticed: Orpheus, on the way back,
so full of the girl, forgot the lyre's luck
that alone had brought them safely to that brink,
and trailing the idle instrument, turned and spoke.
Playing and singing, whistling down that dark,
the whole tensed mind recalling to the work
(each horny finger to its simple trick),
might have kept that final need in check.
Lear and Cordelia, Yeats knew, dare not break
up lines to run offstage and have a talk.
Thus sonnets like lost loves must have their lyric
translation borne on acts of song lest hope-struck
singers drop their instruments and turn
to speaking, all that clear song lost again.

Don't Look Back

How readily it came into his hands,
the lyre, how simply gave itself to song,
the fingers never forced by song's demands—
the need to make it rhyme—to make it wrong.
Now it's an electric guitar he stands
on stage and holds us tranced with all night long,
singing "Sad-Eyed Lady of the Lowlands,"
so full of departure, laboring among
the earthbound farmers and the businessmen,
none of whom know the worth of his creation;
no more than Rilke could have known it then,
seeing, in our new machines, a pure negation,
missing the angels, the old ones minding his pen,
who keep one Orpheus safe in all translation.

This Water

—toward Elyce Fishman-Brothers, 1943-1987

This water rose invisible from the sea.
It gathers in clouds to fall to earth again
as unforeseeable tears at an old Disney movie
and tears at your funeral, Elyce. It returns to the sea
where you've gone, where we hope it finds a way to find you,
bearing a verse Bette Midler sang in *The Rose*,
including the line left out of our little pamphlets;
bearing a verse sung once by Karen Carpenter,
who won our stunned respect by choosing death;
bearing scripture and stories composed or stammered
in stiff shoes, recalcitrant hair, ill-chosen ties
toward you who loved bad poetry and good people.

Bearing toward you the luminous last memoirs
and dying poems of the good Paul Zweig:
prose I was reading the day we learned it had you
(held back in fear of connections? *cancer? Jew?*),
poems I was reading the day the phone rang.
Tears I wept last night on our floral sofa
all through a TV showing of *The Parent Trap*
for my smallest sister's resemblance to Hayley Mills,
for the sisters' having been kept from each other, *secrets*,
for wanting, thirty five years since they saw each other,
to trick my only parents back together.

This weekend in Chicago Ann and I
in all our walking saw how subtly filth
shadows glory down the grandest street—
one more meaning gathered by your death.
Water risen ageless from the sea,
solve each life, all difference in earth.

Packing the Harvard Classics into a Box

Packing the Harvard Classics into a box,
the 1909 set marked "Brooks School for Boys,
Indianapolis," forty-eight books for six bucks,
bought to stop great gaps in the arrays
of books I'd somehow earned (read one by one)
that yawned of greater gaps in my education—
storing them in the rafters till they've won
new space, or old space back, I doom the nation?
I've failed to absorb a great wave of immigration;
it's true, it's sad, it's no cause for hysteria.
Many a Greek remains, in more current translation,
and now there's room for the Library of America.
We'll build a bigger house, with wider shelves;
these old Classics will remain themselves.

Hints from Heloise

Anything can be put to some good use
like keeping a house together, clothes on our backsides,
kids in toys and safe. I mean even this
if you bring it home, where you feed the stove with logs
of newsprint, save odd screws in coffee cans
for when things work loose, save old panty hose
to stuff the pillows you dream on, plastic bags
to keep the dust off, rubber bands to stretch
but not to break while keeping like things together
in the closet, in the attic, amid the trusses
above the garage where you keep the baby things
you still conceive some use for. What is useless
if its burning warms, if it lines, bonds, softens
some contact, brightens the nest? If you bring it home.

River in Winter

The water gains and fails against the ice
that thickens, dwindles by in wet grey lumps,
skins, then seals and downs in snow chill floods
that swell to burst it, bear it heavy down
to dirty ice-jams humping up the narrows
that thicken, dwindle, hiss, disintegrate,
float grey icebergs vanishing by in silence,
thinner, whiter, now as clear as air
that shivers down the perfect next new skin.
We too, all winter, bore another body,
chill and rigid, which we could not bear;
bore its sullen bulk and did not know
what it was, or what there was to do,
or when some spring might come and let us go.

River. Tree.

The great broken willow tilted off the bank
out over water propped on one thick branch
that found a rock and rooted grew to be
our first good reason for coming to live in the house
on the river even after the flood first fall
hollowed out the bank and cut its lifespan.

Alone first winter I watched a red-tailed hawk
perched at the willow's one stretch of open water
throw itself down from the branch and borne on the current
past the tree again fight up onto the ice,
flourish its wings to dry them, fly to the branch
and throw itself into the water, over and over.

Past the far bank, a cornfield overlooked
by pine-dark hills November shot with orange:
We heard a shot then a shot and saw on the bank
a doe, still thrashing. Hunter myself, I watched:
Before he dragged her gutted off he knelt
at the river's edge to wash the blood from his knife.

In the willow this winter, year's first bitter cold,
the pileated woodpecker's great red crest.
Next day, another sign: thick scatter of splinters
over the bank; in the trunk of a flourishing cedar
three great squared-off holes six inches deep,
straight to the hollow heart of the living tree.

NOTES

"The Man Who Broke Up the Dinner Party Answers" was written after a viewing of Judy Chicago's *The Dinner Party.*

"Praise of Hunger, Praise of Food" was written after a reading of Piers Paul Read's *Alive.*

"Villanelle of the Final Report" contains a large amount of found material from Martin Andersen's "Stones for Bread," *The Nation,* May 14, 1983.

"The Throne of the Third Heaven of the Nations Millennium General Assembly" was composed from found material in folk art texts, chiefly Elinor Lander Horwitz's *Contemporary American Folk Artists.*